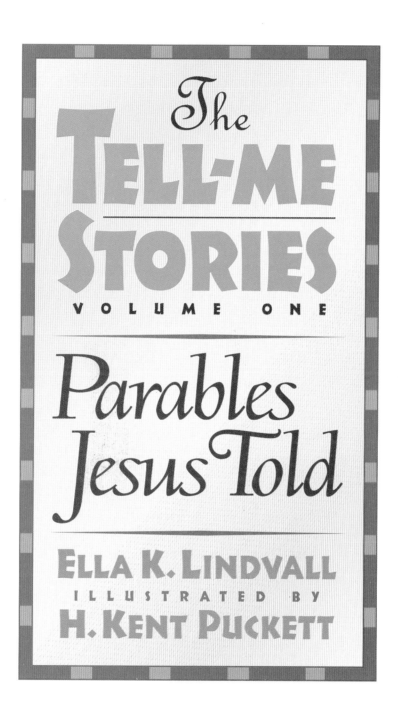

The TELL-ME STORIES

VOLUME ONE

Parables Jesus Told

ELLA K. LINDVALL

ILLUSTRATED BY

H. KENT PUCKETT

Moody Press
Chicago

For Pat

And for Jason

EJ

1 3 5 7 9 10 8 9 4 2

Moody Press, a ministry of Moody Bible Institute, is designed for education, evangelization, and edification. If we may assist you in knowing more about Christ and the Christian life, please write us without obligation: Moody Press, c/o MLM, Chicago, Illinois 60610.

Contents

The Foolish Farmer
(Luke 12:16–21)

One day Jesus told a story. This is what He said:

Once upon a time there was a farmer. He had a big garden. Lots of wheat plants grew in his garden.

He had many helpers.
They all worked for him.

He had a nice house.
He had many pennies.

Now, God gave him his garden.
But the farmer didn't think about that.

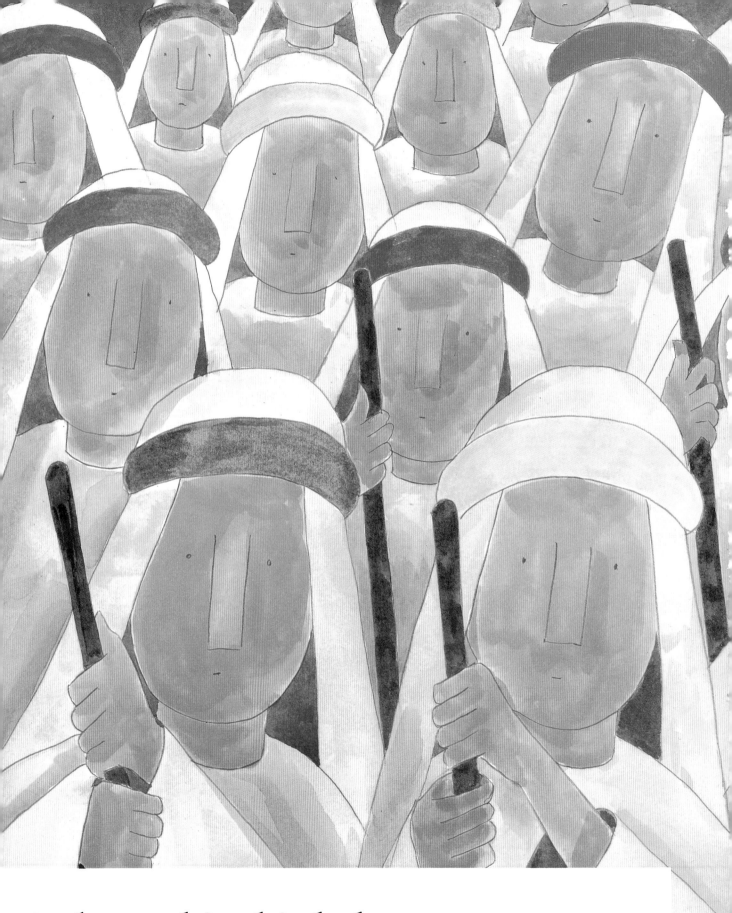

God gave him his helpers.
But the farmer didn't think about that.

God gave him his house.
But the farmer didn't think about that.

God gave him his pennies.
But the farmer didn't think about that.

One day he said,
"Look at my big garden.
Look at all my wheat plants.
It is time to cut down the wheat.
But where shall I put it?
My barns are too little."

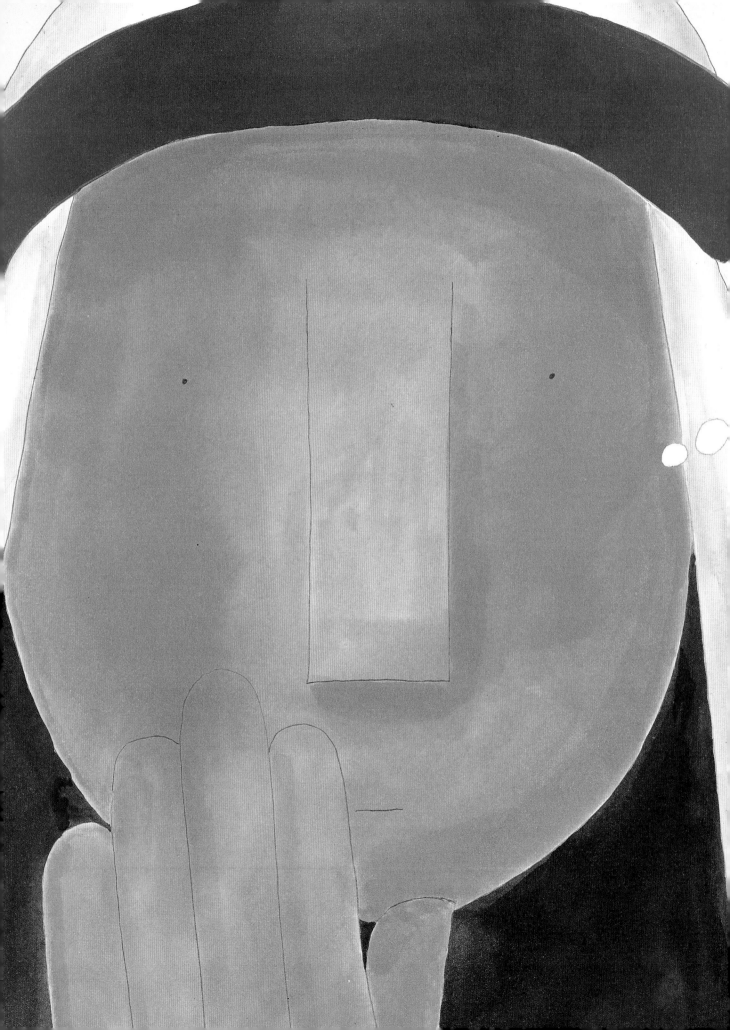

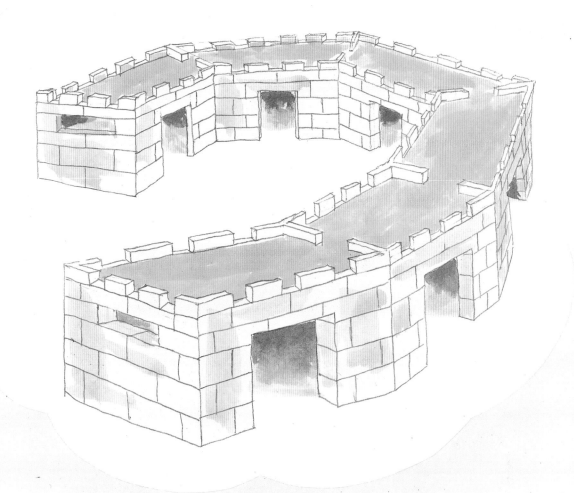

The farmer thought
and thought and thought.
He said, "I know!
I will tear down my barns.
I will build bigger barns.
Then I will have room
for all my wheat."

The farmer
was still thinking.
He said, "And THEN
I will not work anymore.
I will eat.
I will drink.
I will play every day
for a long, long time."

But the farmer
would not live
a long, long time.
He didn't think about that.

Somebody else
would get the things in his barns.
He didn't think about that.

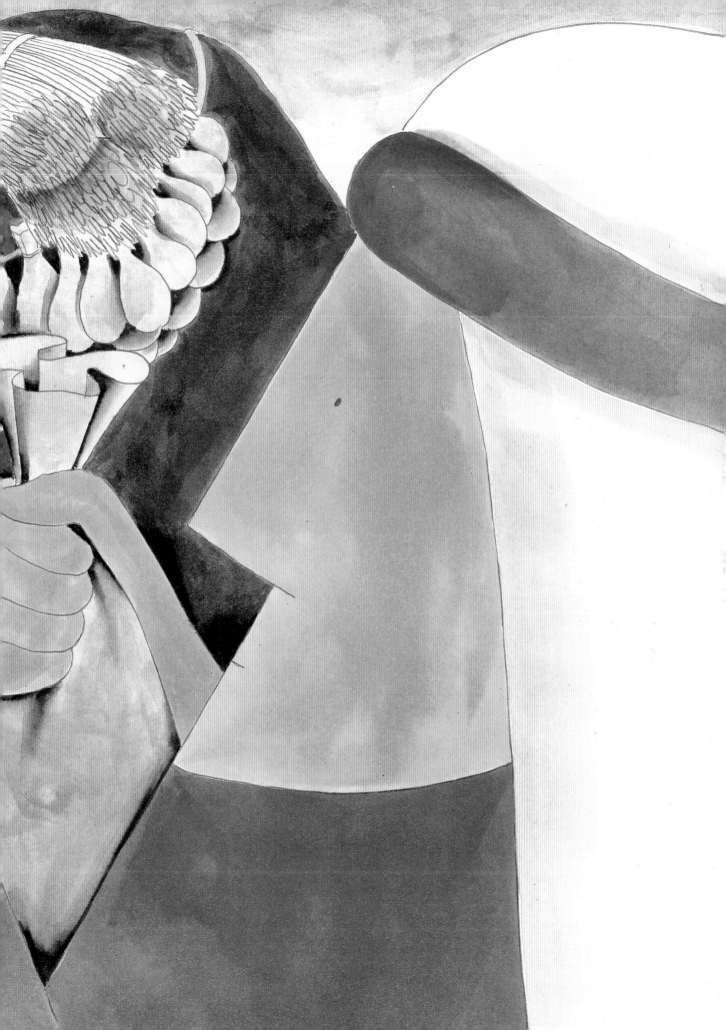

He had many things,
but he was not
one of God's friends.
He didn't think about that.
He was a foolish, foolish farmer.

What did you learn?

It's better to be God's friend than to have a lot of things.

The Sheep That Was Lost
(Luke 15:3–7)

One day Jesus told a story.
This is what He said:

Once upon a time
there was a man
who had some sheep.
He loved his sheep.

Every day
the man took his sheep
out to a grassy hill.
The sheep ate the grass.
The sheep were happy.

Every night
the man took his sheep
back home.
Every night
the man said,
"Are all my sheep here?"

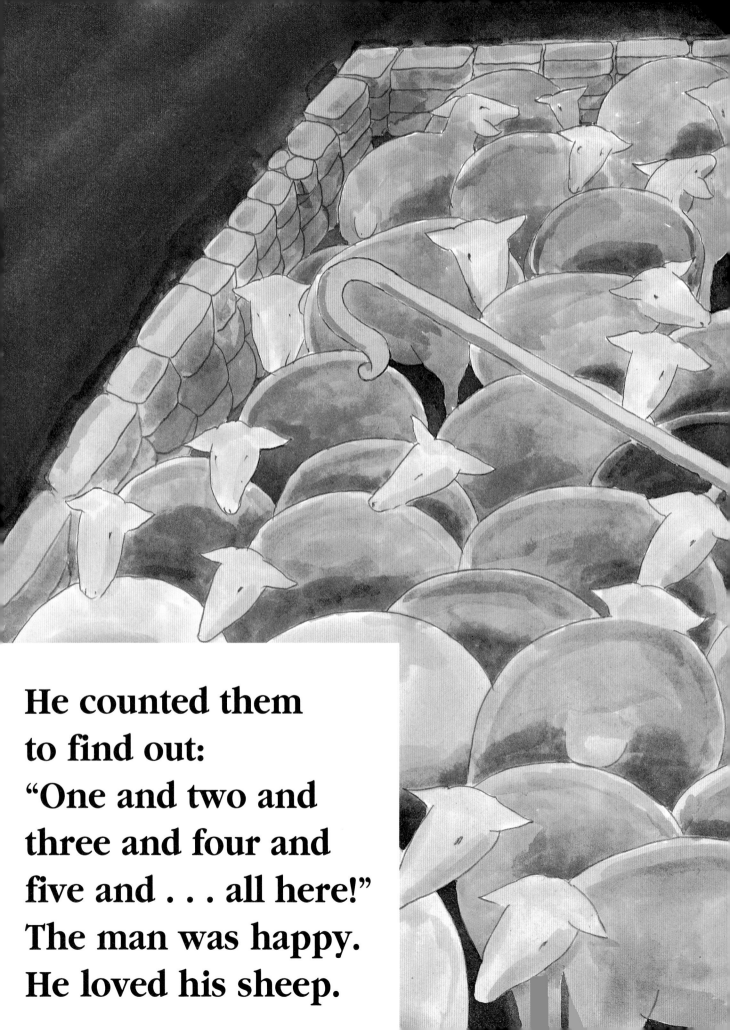

He counted them
to find out:
"One and two and
three and four and
five and . . . all here!"
The man was happy.
He loved his sheep.

But one day
something happened.
In the morning,
the man took his sheep
out to a grassy hill.
The sheep ate the grass.
The sheep were happy.

**At night he took them home.
He said, "Are all my sheep here?"
He counted them to find out:**

"One and two and three and four and . . ."

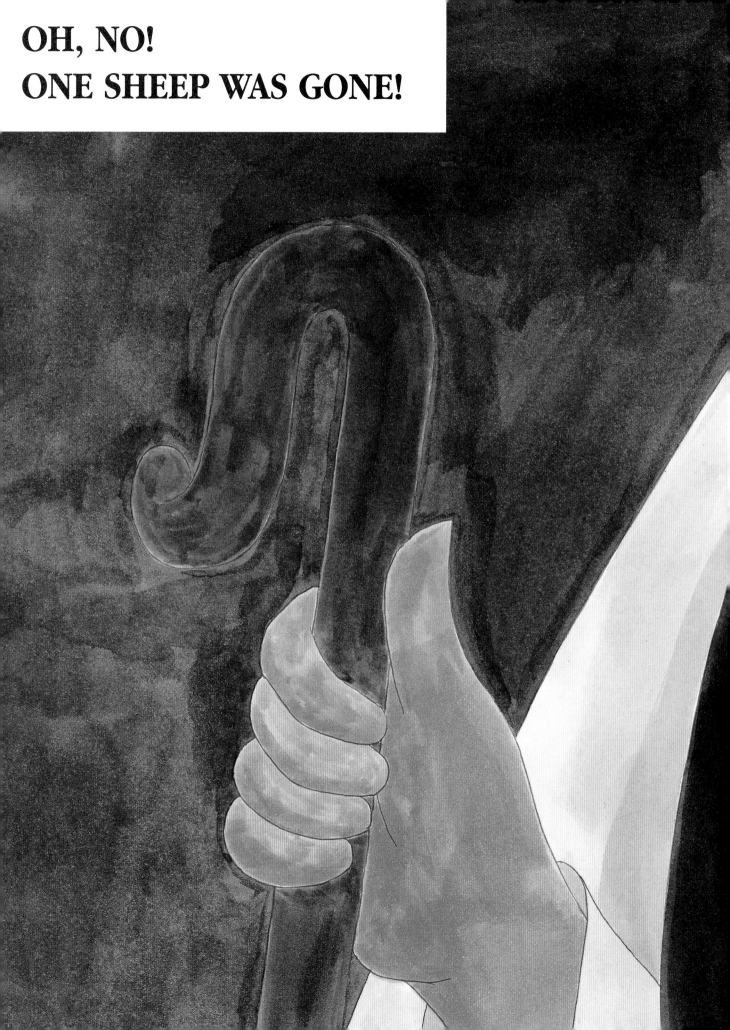

The man ran back
to the grassy hill.
He loved that sheep.
He looked here.
No sheep.
He looked there.
No sheep.
He looked this way.
No sheep.
He looked that way.
No sheep.
But then—

what was that?
It was something white.
It looked like . . . it WAS!
It was his lost sheep!

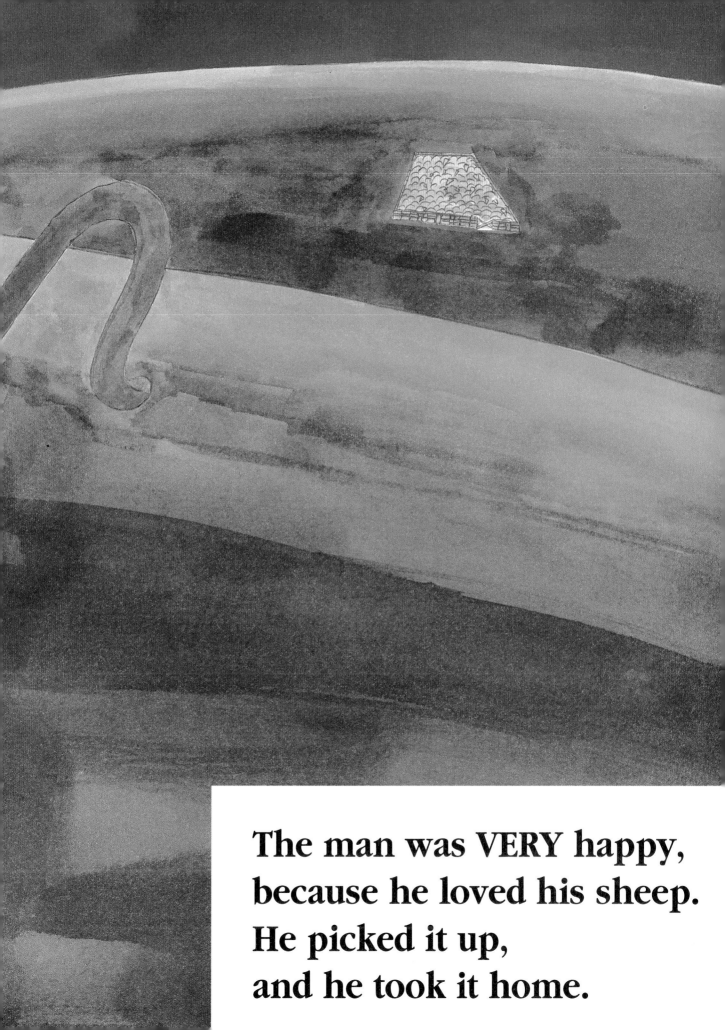

The man was VERY happy,
because he loved his sheep.
He picked it up,
and he took it home.

Then the man called his friends.
He said, "Be happy with me!
I have found my lost sheep."

And the Lord said,
when a mommy or a daddy
or a boy or a girl says,
"Yes! *I* will love Jesus,"
then GOD is happy,
because God loves people.

What did you learn?

God loves YOU,
and you can make Him happy.
Love the Lord Jesus.
Do what He says.

The People Helper Who Wouldn't Help
(Luke 18:1-8)

One day Jesus told a story.
This is what He said:

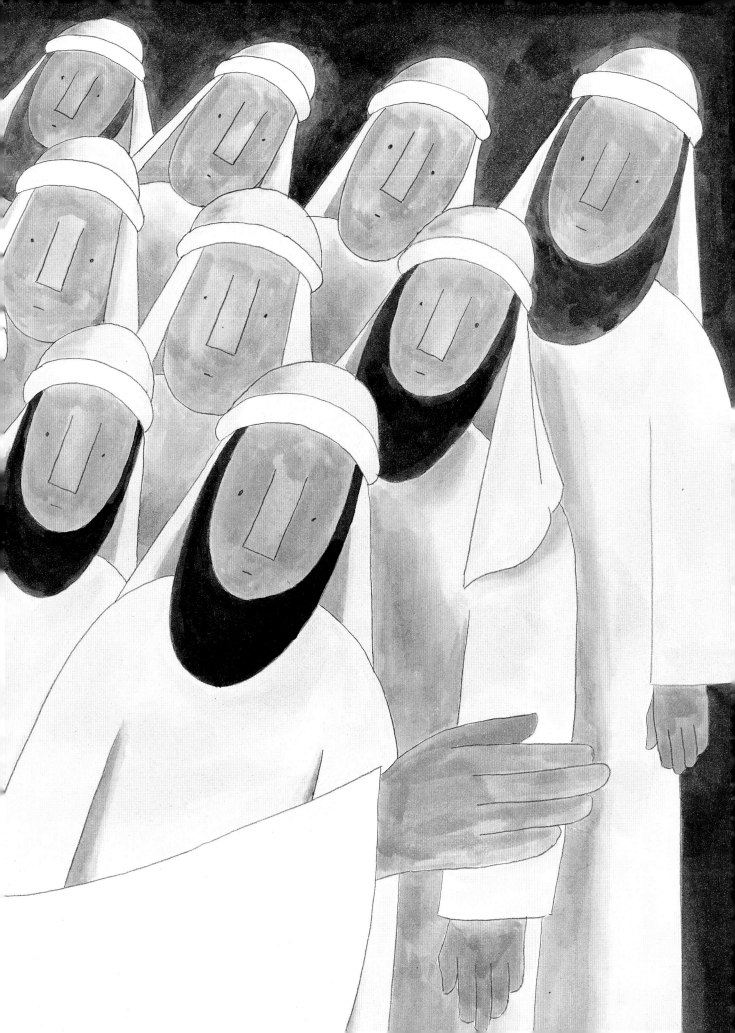

Once upon a time
there was a people helper.
But he was not
a good people helper.

He didn't try to do
what God wanted.
He didn't try to do
what people wanted.
He just did
what HE wanted.

One day a lady came
to his house.
She said, "Please help me."

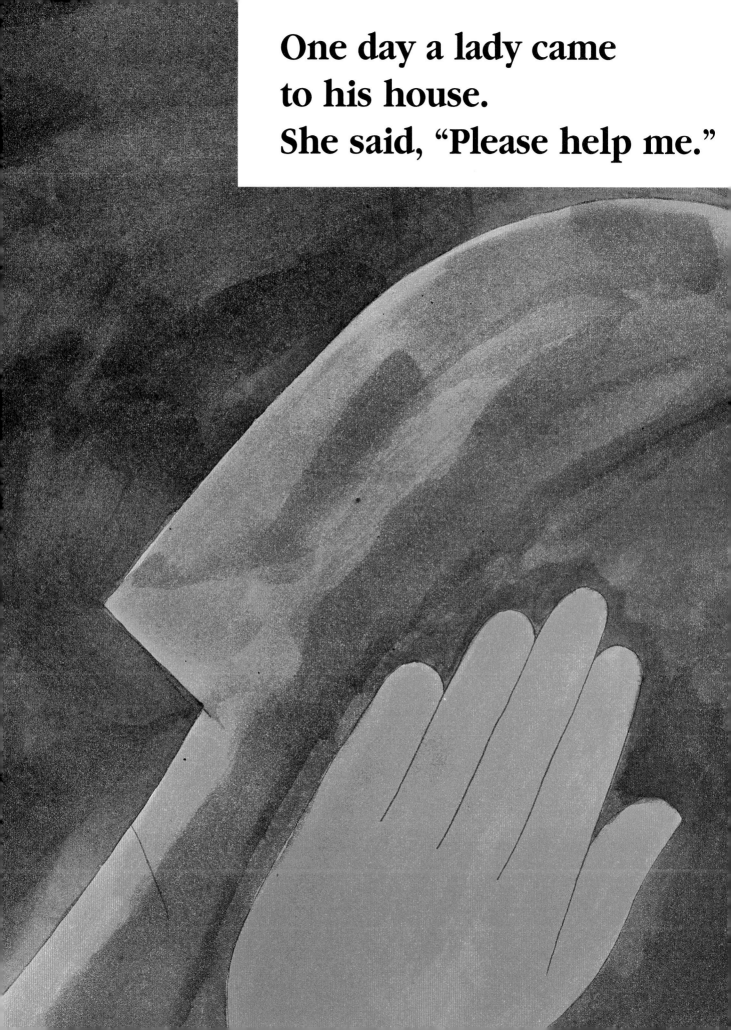

But the people helper
wouldn't help.
He wouldn't listen.

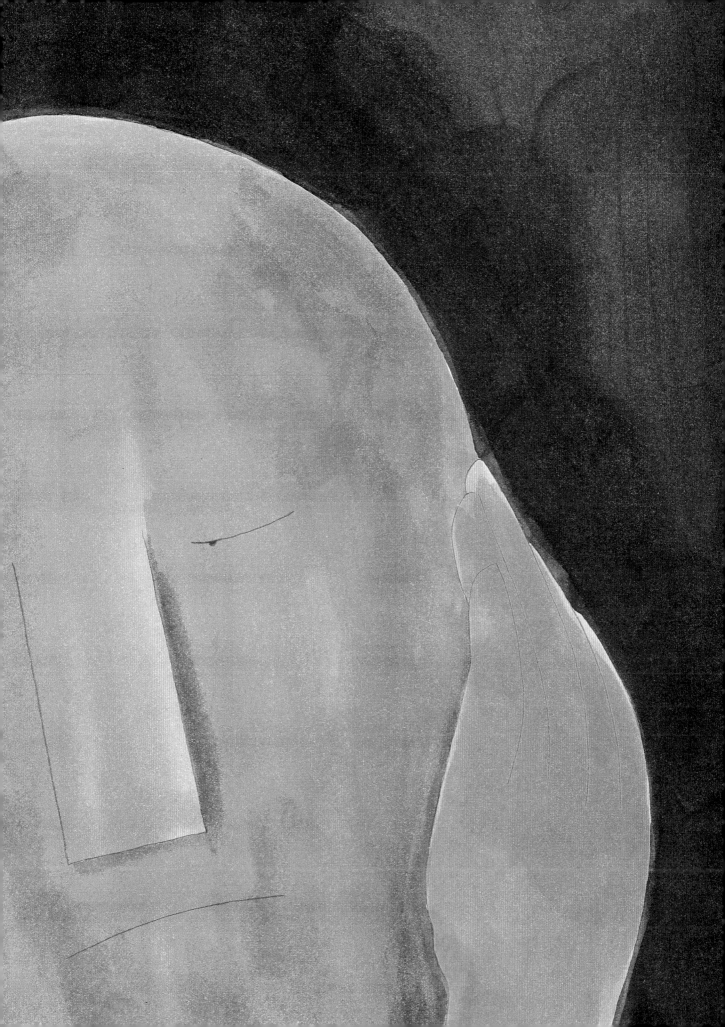

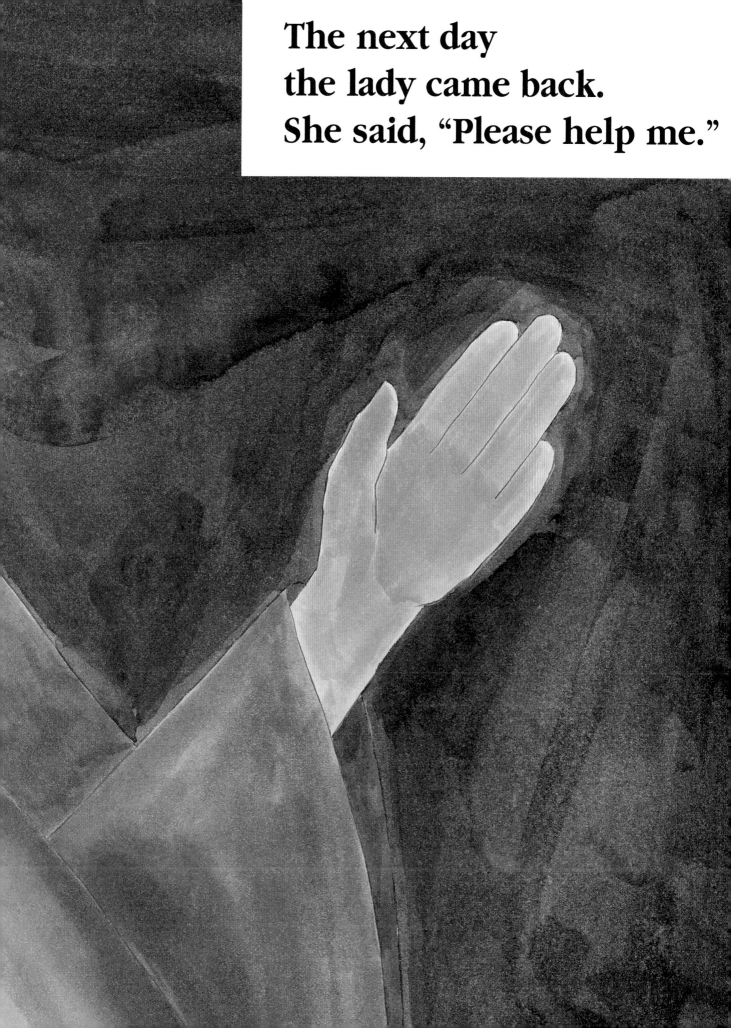

The next day
the lady came back.
She said, "Please help me."

But the people helper
wouldn't help.
He wouldn't listen.

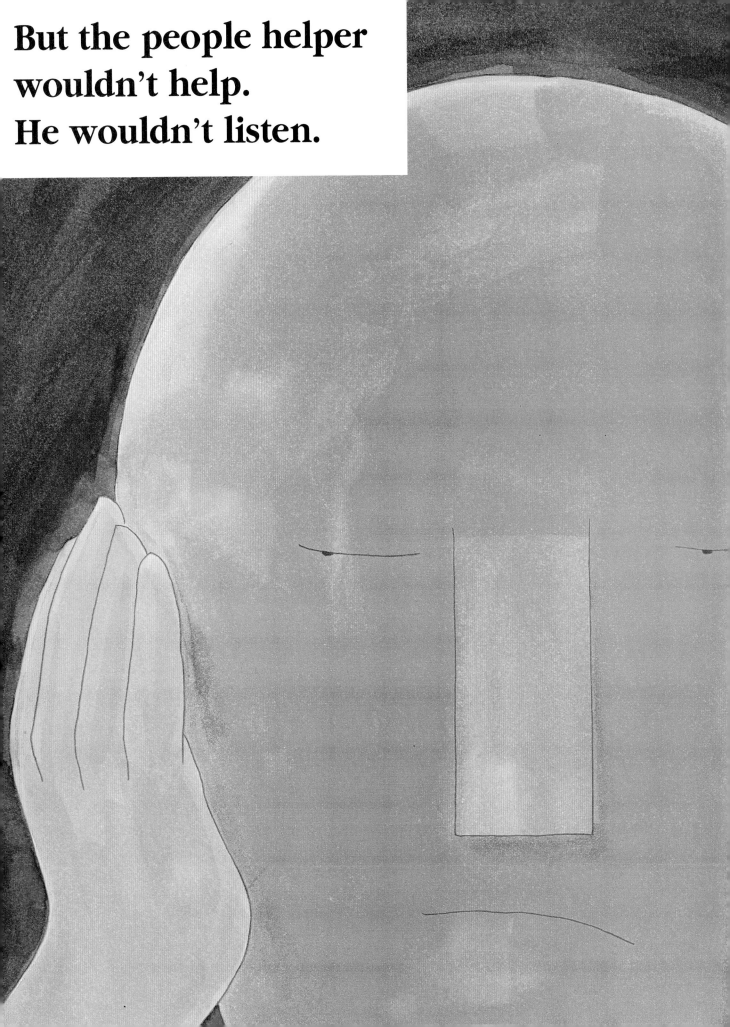

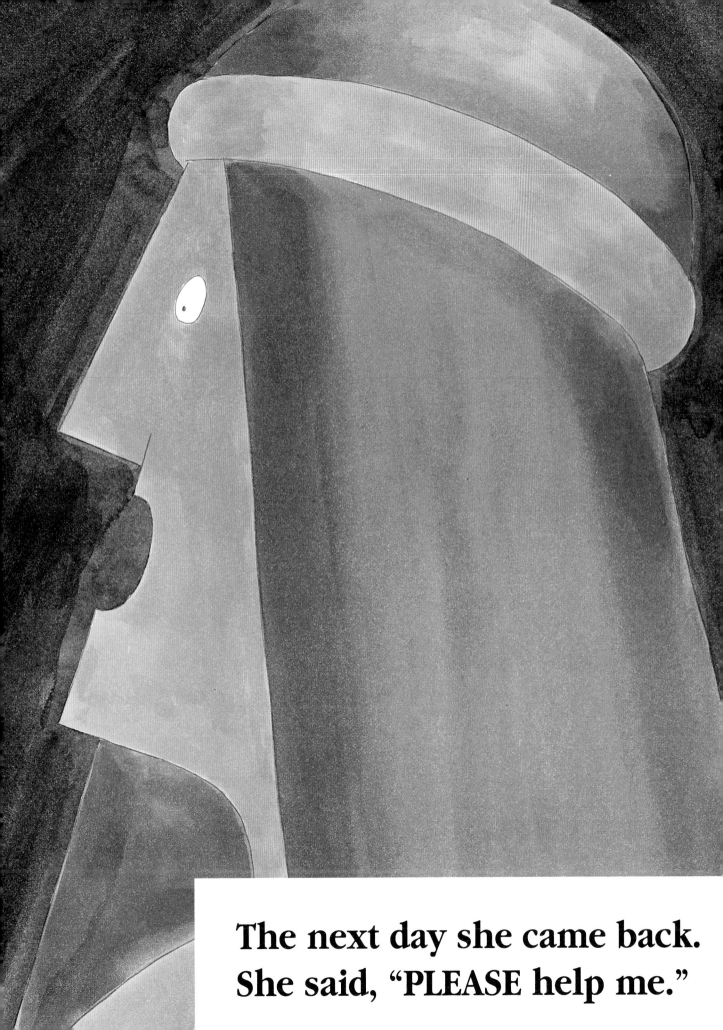

The next day she came back.
She said, "PLEASE help me."

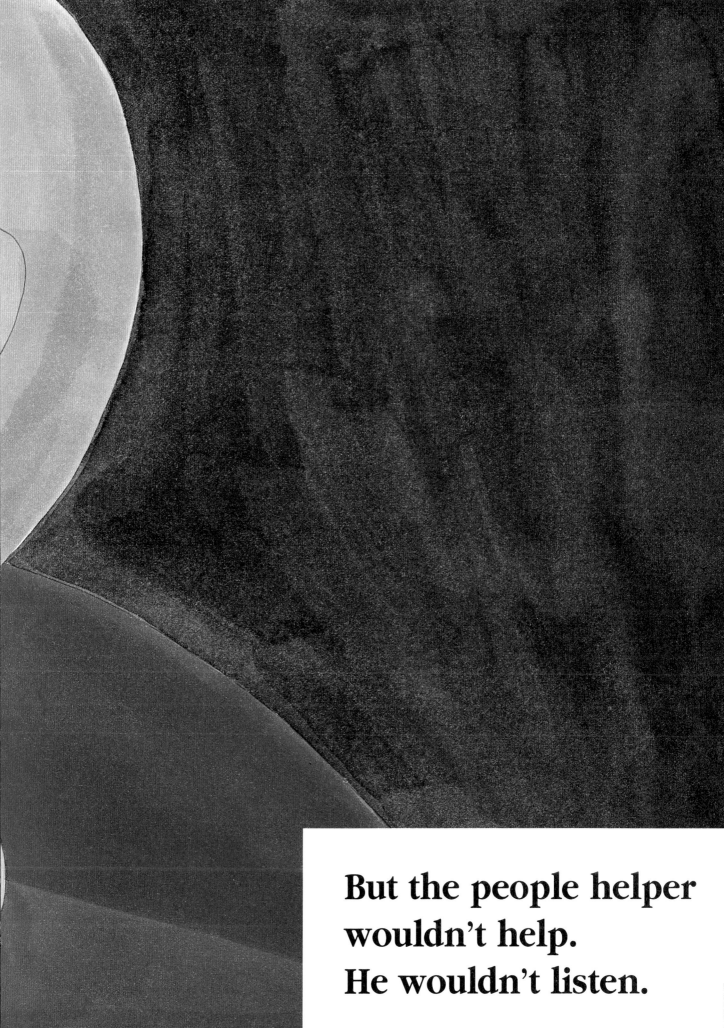

But the people helper
wouldn't help.
He wouldn't listen.

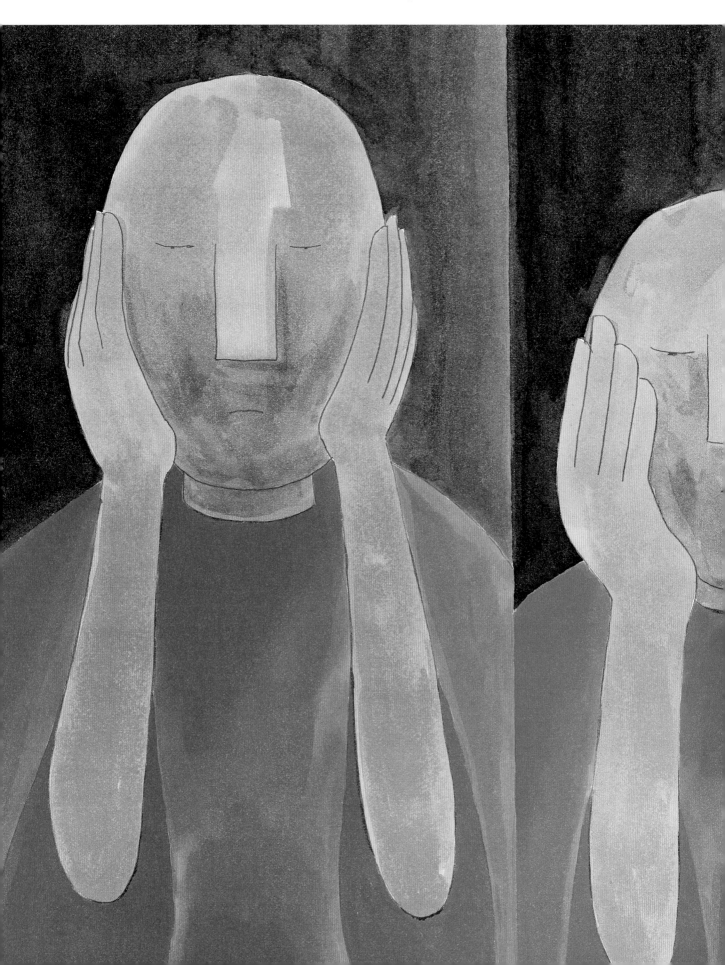

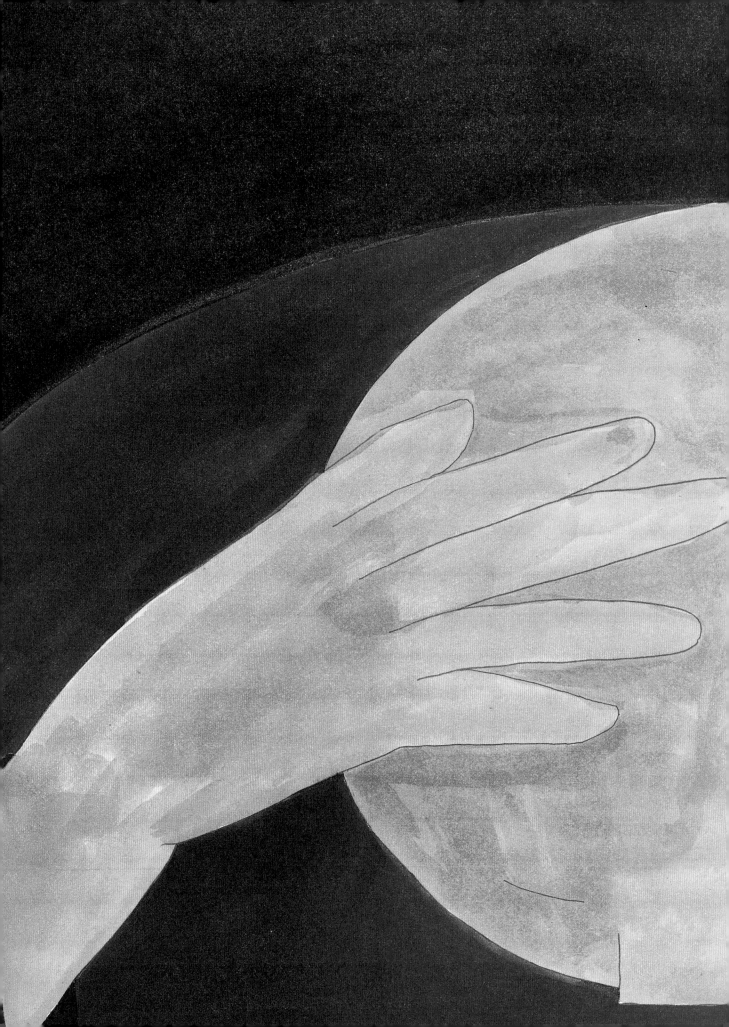

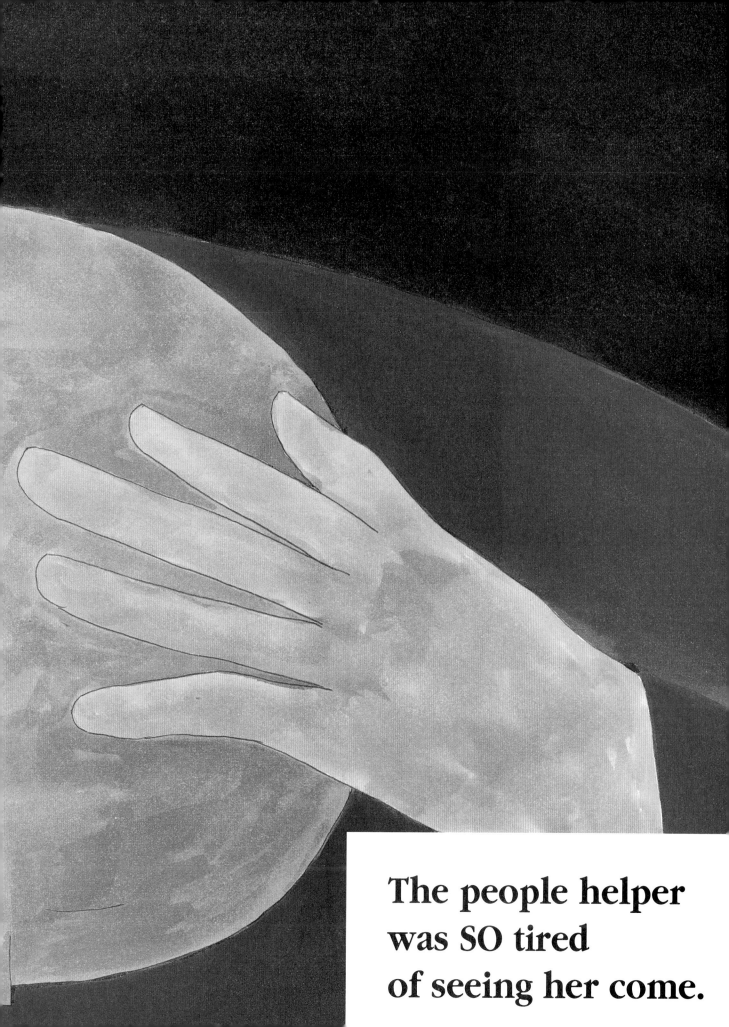

The people helper
was SO tired
of seeing her come.

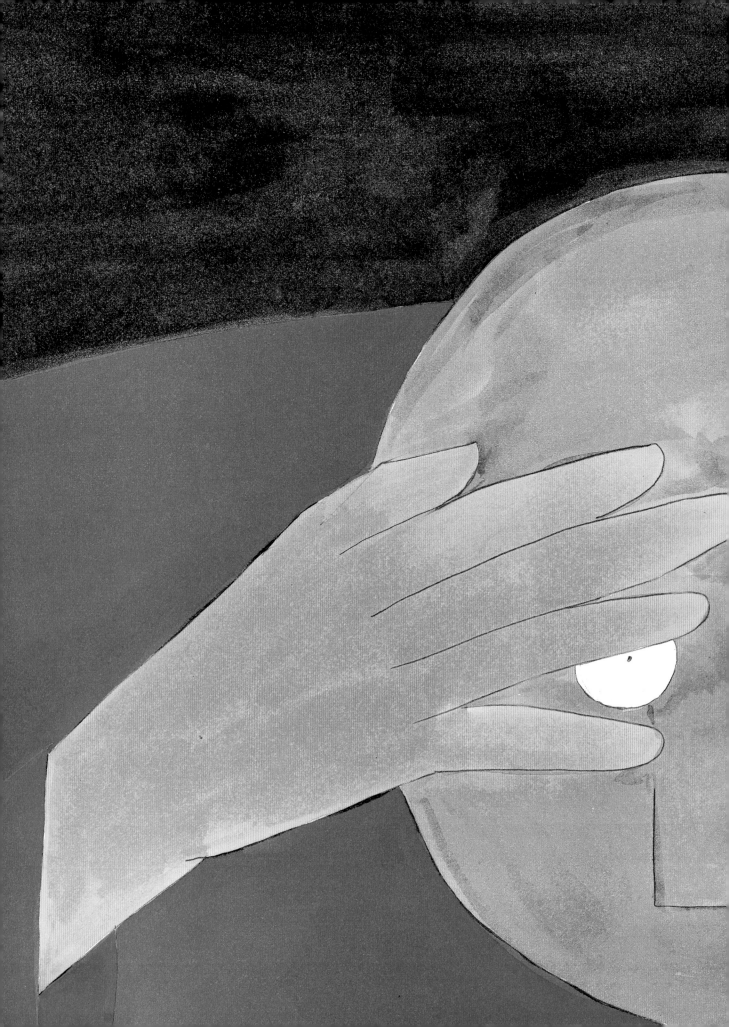

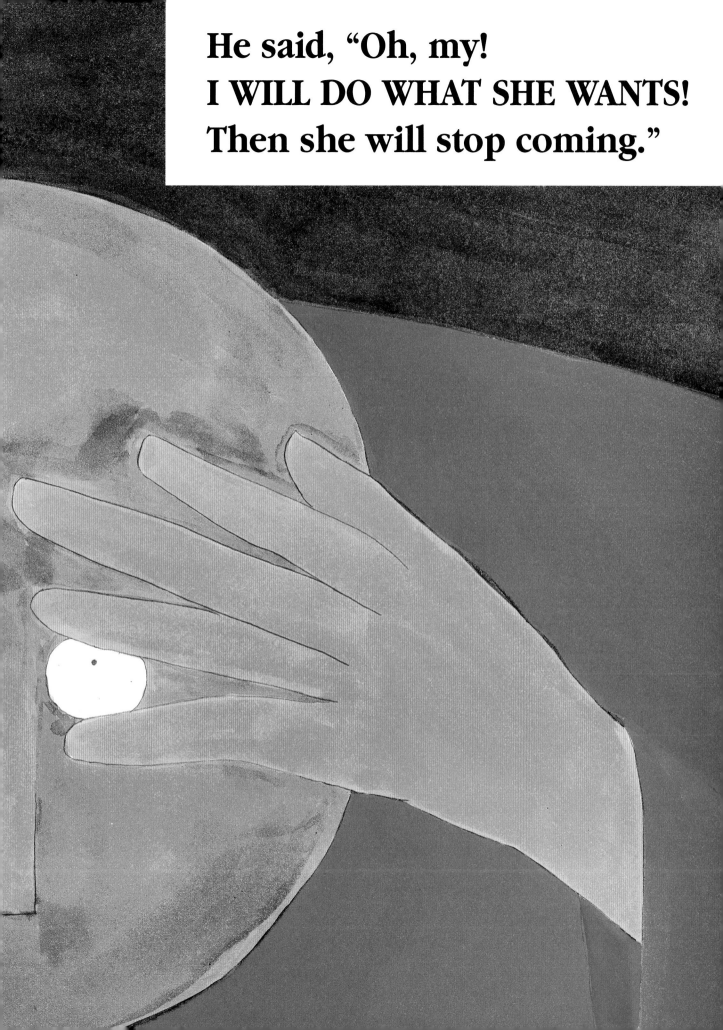

Did you hear
what the people helper said?
He was not a good man.
He helped the lady
just so she wouldn't
bother him.

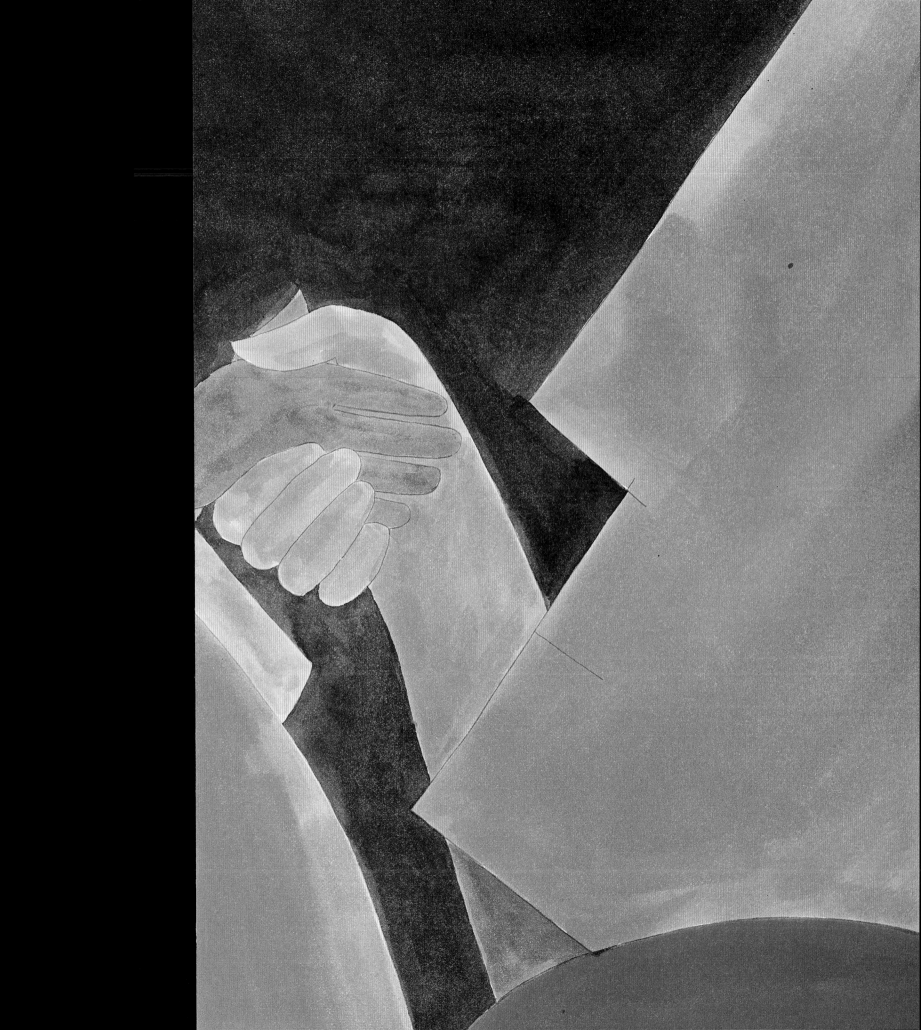

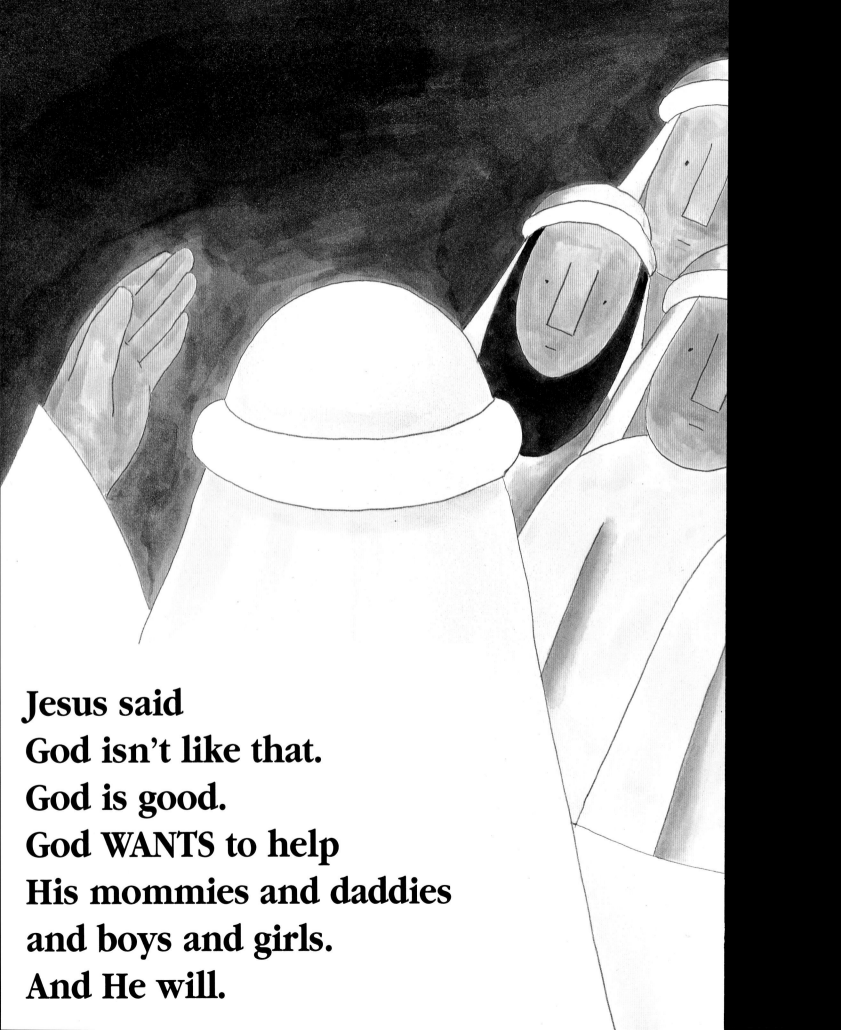

**Jesus said
God isn't like that.
God is good.
God WANTS to help
His mommies and daddies
and boys and girls.
And He will.**

What did you learn?

Who is the best people helper?
God is!
And He likes you.
He LIKES to see you come.
He listens.

Two Men Who Talked to God
(Luke 18: 9-14)

**One day Jesus told a story.
This is what He said.**

Up, up, up, and up,
two men went up the steps
into the temple-church.

They wanted to talk to God.

He said,
"Thank You, God,
that I'm better
than other people.

I do only good things.
I even give pennies
to the temple-church."

And then he saw
the other man.

He said, "THAT man
TAKES PENNIES
AWAY FROM PEOPLE.
I never do that."
That was what he said.

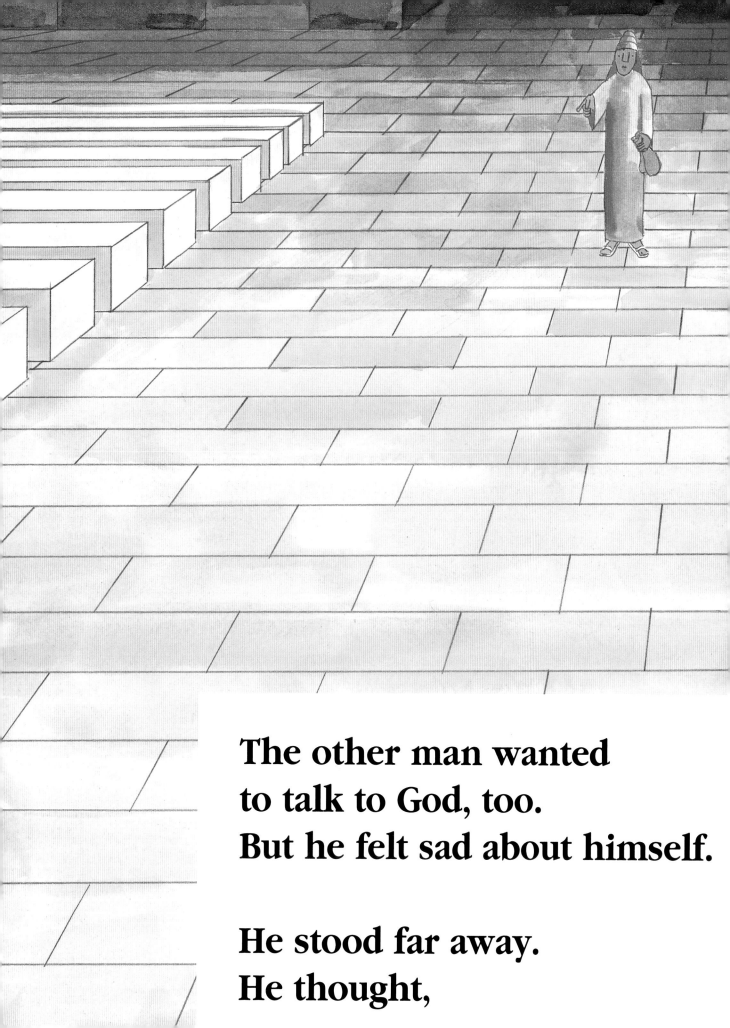

The other man wanted
to talk to God, too.
But he felt sad about himself.

He stood far away.
He thought,

"God is not pleased with me.
I have done wrong things.
I am ashamed
even to look up
to where God is."
That was what he thought.

Then he said,
"O God,
I need help.
I need You
to forgive me
for not making
You happy."

Now, God was pleased
to hear that kind of prayer.
God did forgive him.
And the man went home.

The first man—
remember him?—
the first man
thought he was good.
But he wasn't.
He wasn't because—

there just AREN'T any
good-all-the-time people.
EVERYBODY
does things that are wrong.
EVERYBODY
needs to tell Jesus,
"I'm sorry."

What did you learn?

Even nice people
need to say,
"Lord Jesus, I've done wrong.
Please forgive me."
And He will.

Two Men and Their Houses
(Matthew 7:24-27)

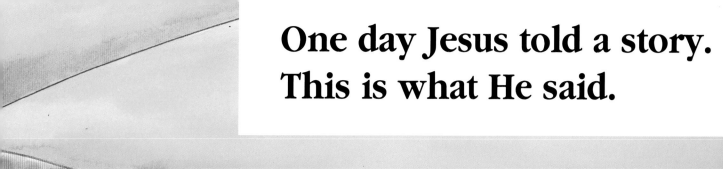

One day Jesus told a story.
This is what He said.

BANG!
BANG!
BANG-ETY BANG!
A man was building a house.

BANG!
BANG!
Up went the walls.
BANG!
BANG!
On went the roof.

The man
was building
his house
on a big rock.
And that was
a good thing,
because—

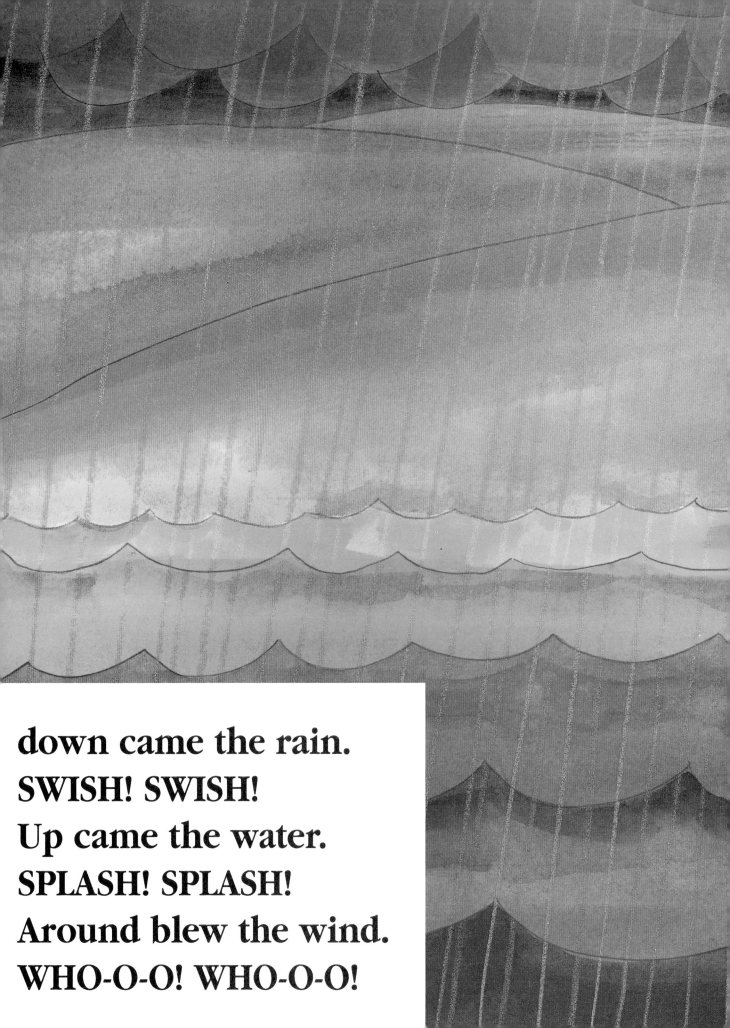

down came the rain.
SWISH! SWISH!
Up came the water.
SPLASH! SPLASH!
Around blew the wind.
WHO-O-O! WHO-O-O!

But all the rain
and all the water
and all the wind
didn't hurt that house
one bit.

Wasn't the man wise
to build his house
on a rock?

BANG!
BANG!
BANG-ETY BANG!
Another man
was building
a house.

BANG!
BANG!
Up went the walls.
BANG!
BANG!
On went the roof.

This man
was building
his house
on some sand.
And that WASN'T
a good thing,
because—

down came the rain.
SWISH! SWISH!
Up came the water.
SPLASH! SPLASH!
Around blew the wind.
WHO-O-O! WHO-O-O!

The sand washed away,
and down went the house.
CRACK-ETY!
CRASH-ETY!
SMASH-ETY!
BONG!

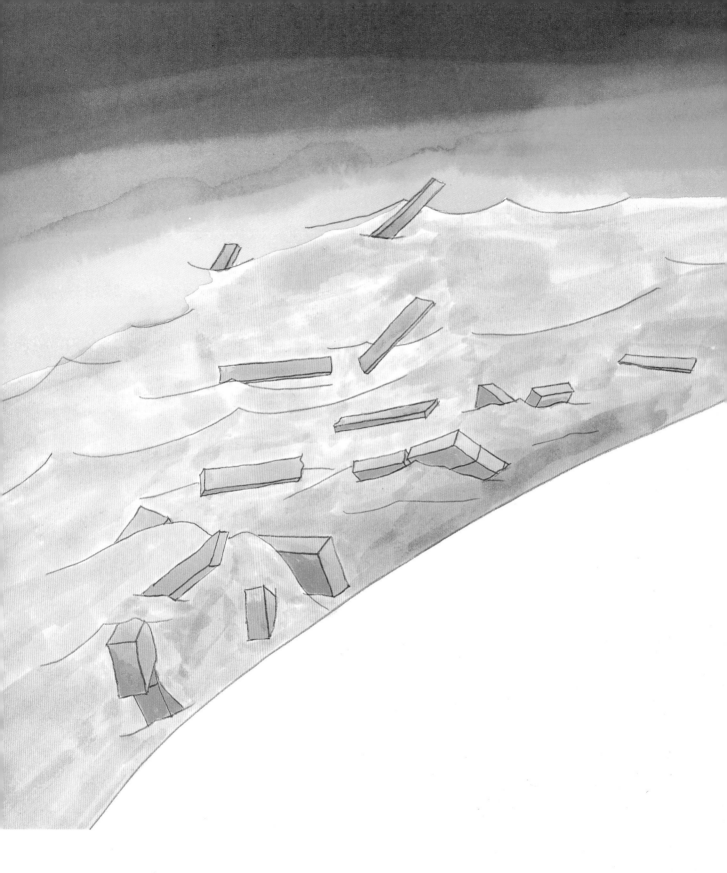

**Wasn't that man foolish
to build his house
on SAND?**

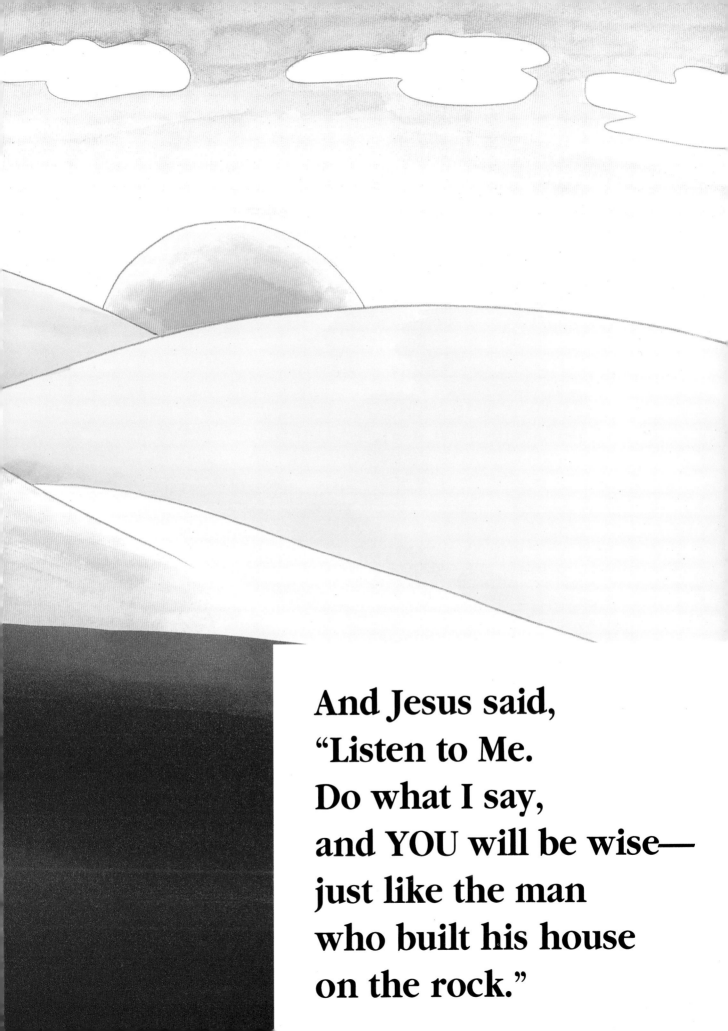

And Jesus said,
"Listen to Me.
Do what I say,
and YOU will be wise—
just like the man
who built his house
on the rock."

What did you learn?

Wise boys and girls
and wise mommies and daddies
do what Jesus says.